THE MONTREAL CANADIENS

ANDREW LUKE

childsworld.com

Published by The Child's World®
800-599-READ • www.childsworld.com

Copyright © 2026 by The Child's World®
All rights reserved. No part of this book may be reproduced or utilized in any form or by any means without written permission from the publisher.

Photography Credits
Cover: ©Victor Munhoz/NHLI/Getty Images; page 5: ©Minas Panagiotakis/Getty Images Sport/Getty Images; page 6: ©UPI/Bettmann Archive/Getty Images; page 9: ©Gerry Angus/Icon Sportswire/Getty Images; page 10: ©Vincent Ethier/Icon Sportswire/Getty Images; page 12: ©David Kirouac/Icon Sportswire/Getty Images; page 12: ©Rich Graessle/NHLI/Getty Images; page 13: ©Richard Wolowicz/Getty Images Sport/Getty Images; page 13: ©Michell Layton/Getty Images Sport/Getty Images; page 14: ©Minas Panagiotakis/Getty Images Sport/Getty Images; page 16: ©Bruce Bennett Studios/Getty Images Studios/Getty Images; page 16: ©Denis Brodeur/NHLI/Getty Images; page 17: ©Focus on Sport/Getty Images Sport/Getty Images; page 17: ©Focus on Sport/Getty Images Sport/Getty Images; page 18: ©Bruce Bennett Studios/Getty Images Studios/Getty Images; page 18: ©Denis Brodeur/NHLI/Getty Images; page 19: ©Bruce Bennett Studios/Getty Images Studios/Getty Images; page 19: ©Andre Pichette/Bruce Bennett/Getty Images: page 20: ©Minas Panagiotakis/Getty Images Sport/Getty Images; page 20: ©Minas Panagiotakis/Getty Images Sport/Getty Images; page 21: ©Minas Panagiotakis/Getty Images Sport/Getty Images; page 21: ©Vitor Munhoz/NHLI/Getty Images; page 22: ©Pictorial Parade/Archive Photos/Getty Images; page 23: ©Bruce Bennett Studios/Getty Images Studios/Getty Images; page 25: ©Denis Brodeur/NHLI/Getty Images; page 26: ©Bruce Bennett Studios/Getty Images Studios/Getty Images; page 29: ©Denis Brodeur/NHLI/Getty Images

ISBN Information
9781503870680 (Reinforced Library Binding)
9781503871922 (Portable Document Format)
9781503873162 (Online Multi-user eBook)
9781503874404 (Electronic Publication)

LCCN
2024950296

Printed in the United States of America

ABOUT THE AUTHOR
Andrew Luke is a former journalist-turned-freelance writer. He has written about everything from chefs to China, but he focuses primarily on sports. Andrew is a lifelong fan of all sports, especially hockey. He lives in sunny Florida, where he enjoys spending time with his wife and kids.

CONTENTS

Go Canadiens! . . . 4
Becoming the Canadiens . . . 7
By the Numbers . . . 8
Game Night . . . 11
Uniforms . . . 12
Team Spirit . . . 15
Heroes of History . . . 16
Big Days . . . 18
Modern-Day Marvels . . . 20
The G.O.A.T. . . . 23
The Big Game . . . 24
Amazing Feats . . . 27
All-Time Best . . . 28

Glossary . . . 30
Fast Facts . . . 31
One Stride Further . . . 31
Find Out More . . . 32
Index . . . 32

Go Canadiens!

The Montreal Canadiens are the oldest team in the National Hockey League (NHL). In the French-speaking city of Montreal, the hockey team is called Le Club de Hockey Canadien. The word *Canadiens* is spelled with an "e" because it's French for "Canadians." Montreal plays in the NHL's Atlantic **Division**. It has also won the most championships, with 22 NHL Stanley Cup victories.

Eastern Conference • Atlantic Division

Boston Bruins	Detroit Red Wings	**Montreal Canadiens**	Tampa Bay Lightning
Buffalo Sabres	Florida Panthers	Ottawa Senators	Toronto Maple Leafs

The Canadiens celebrate a win over the St. Louis Blues early in the 2024–2025 season.

Canadiens players celebrate their Stanley Cup win with Clarence Campbell, president of the NHL, in 1969.

Becoming the Canadiens

The Canadiens were founded in 1909 by John Ambrose O'Brien. Montreal started out in the Canadian Hockey Association. Then they joined the National Hockey Association (NHA). This league eventually became the National Hockey League (NHL). The Canadiens have won 24 championships. Two of them were before the NHL officially started using the Stanley Cup as its trophy in 1927. Montreal has had two **dynasty** periods. From 1956 through 1960, they won five Stanley Cups in a row with star players such as Jean Béliveau and Jacques Plante. Another great streak came from 1976 through 1979, when they won four in a row. Those teams were led by **Hall of Fame** players Guy Lafleur and Larry Robinson.

By the Numbers

The Canadiens have had a lot of success on the ice. Here are just a few interesting facts:

 The Canadiens have made the **playoffs** in 85 seasons, more than any other team in the league. **85**

 Fifty-seven Montreal players are in the Hockey Hall of Fame. That is the third-most of all teams. **57**

 The Canadiens have retired 18 player jerseys, the most in the league. **18**

 On March 3, 1920, the Canadiens scored 16 goals in one game. That is an NHL record that still stands. **16**

The Canadiens have won 440 of their 761 playoff games. ▶

Bell Centre is a sea of red at every Canadiens game. The team had the highest average home attendance in the NHL in the 2022–2023 season.

Game Night

Montreal plays its home games at the Bell Centre, which opened in 1996. It took three years to build and can hold more than 21,000 fans. The building is considered one of the loudest in the NHL because Canadiens games are sold out every night. The Bell Centre replaced one of the most loved buildings in hockey, the Montreal Forum. The Forum was home to the team from 1926 to 1996. The Forum still stands on the corner of the city's Sainte-Catherine and Atwater Streets. It is now a movie theater and entertainment complex.

We're Proudly French

Fans cheer "Go Habs Go!" during games. The nickname "Habs" comes from the French word *habitants,* which means "residents." It is a reference to early French settlers in Quebec. The Canadiens have a strong French heritage and have always looked for French-Canadian players, including Guy Lafleur and Jean Béliveau. They also prefer coaches who can speak French.

Uniforms

HOME

AWAY

Special Mask

Carey Price wore a custom-made mask for the Montreal Canadiens' Centennial Game against the Boston Bruins at the Bell Centre on December 4, 2009. The mask was designed to honor the Canadiens' 100th anniversary. It featured several legendary Hall of Fame goalies, including Georges Vezina, Patrick Roy, and Gump Worsley. It also displayed the various logos used by the team over the years. The back listed all of the Canadiens' Stanley Cup victories.

Truly Weird

Many hockey fans dream of skating and playing with their favorite players, but few get the chance. In 2006, a Canadiens fan known only as Raphael decided to make his own opportunity. One day in the middle of the season, Raphael showed up at the team's training facility during practice. He brought his own helmet, gloves, stick, and skates. Somehow, he managed to hop on the ice to join practice! He picked up a puck and took two shots on goalie José Théodore. He was unable to score before security dragged him off the ice, but at least he took his shot!

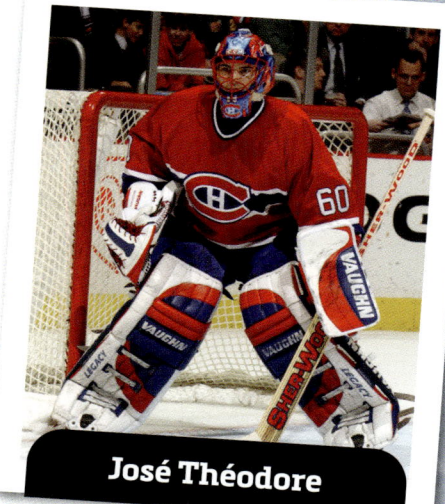

José Théodore

Team Spirit

Montreal once had a baseball team called the Expos. Their mascot was a big orange creature named Youppi!, which means "yippee" in French. He has his own display at the Baseball Hall of Fame in Cooperstown, New York. When the Expos moved to Washington, DC, in 2005 and became the Washington Nationals, Youppi! stayed in Montreal and got a new job with the Canadiens. Now he wears a Canadiens jersey with his trademark "!" in place of a number and entertains fans at the Bell Centre. When the Canadiens are winning late in games, he often leads them in a chant of "Olé!, Olé!, Olé!"

◀ **Youppi! is the first and only North American mascot to switch from one sport to another.**

Heroes of History

Jean Béliveau
Center | 1950–1971

Jean Béliveau played all 20 seasons of his Hall of Fame career in Montreal. He won the Hart Trophy as the NHL's Most Valuable Player (MVP) in 1956. He also won the Art Ross Trophy as the league's scoring leader that year. In 1964, he added a second Hart Trophy to his collection. Béliveau was also a 10-time NHL All-Star. He scored 507 career goals. Béliveau served as team captain from 1961 until he retired 10 years later. The 10-time Stanley Cup champion was beloved by the fans and is one of the team's most admired figures.

Guy Lafleur
Right Wing | 1972–1985

Guy Lafleur won three-straight Art Ross Trophies from 1976 to 1978. In two of those seasons, he also won the Hart Trophy as the NHL MVP. Lafleur played the first 14 of his 17 NHL seasons in Montreal. He helped lead the Habs to five Stanley Cups. Fans would rise to their feet with excitement when Lafleur got the puck and streaked down the ice, his long blond hair flowing famously behind him. Lafleur scored 518 goals in a Montreal uniform, joining Béliveau as one of only three Canadiens with more than 500 career goals as a Hab.

Larry Robinson
Defenseman | 1972–1989

At 6 feet, 4 inches (1.93 meters) and 225 pounds (102 kilograms), Larry Robinson was a force on the ice for Montreal throughout the 1970s and 1980s. A six-time NHL All-Star and six-time Stanley Cup winner, Robinson shut down the other team's forwards and made life easier for his goaltenders. He could also help out at the other end of the ice. Robinson's 958 career points rank ninth in NHL history for scoring by a defenseman.

Patrick Roy
Goaltender | 1985–1995

Patrick Roy burst onto the NHL scene as a rookie in the 1985–1986 season. Throughout that magical season, he led the Canadiens on a surprising run to a Stanley Cup win. The 20-year-old goalie was named the Conn Smythe Trophy winner as the Stanley Cup playoffs MVP. Roy also won 10 overtime games in the 1993 playoffs and led Montreal to a Stanley Cup victory. He won the Vezina Trophy as the league's best goalie three times, in 1989, 1990, and 1992. Roy also made six All-Star teams.

Big Days

APRIL 20, 1984

Known as the Good Friday Massacre, a second-round playoff series game against the **rival** Quebec Nordiques shows just how physical hockey can be. A total of 11 players are ejected, and 252 **penalty** minutes are given out.

The Canadiens win game two of the Stanley Cup Final after a rare **illegal stick** penalty on the Los Angeles Kings' Marty McSorley. Montreal goes on to win the Cup.

JUNE 3, 1993

DECEMBER 2, 1995

Patrick Roy demands to be traded after he felt he was treated badly by his coach during a game against Detroit. Four days later, the two-time Cup winner is traded to the Colorado Avalanche, where he goes on to win two more Stanley Cups. Montreal hasn't won one since.

Team captain Saku Koivu returns to play after a long battle with cancer. The fans jump to their feet and clap for him for five-straight minutes.

APRIL 9, 2002

19

Modern-Day Marvels

Nick Suzuki
Center | 2019–Present

Nick Suzuki has played his whole NHL career in Montreal, but he didn't start out with the Canadiens. Las Vegas chose him in the NHL Draft, but he never played for the Golden Knights, and they traded him to Montreal a year later. He made his debut at the Bell Centre to start the 2019 season. Suzuki increased his goal total in each of his first five seasons, including 33 goals in 2023–2024. He was named captain of the Habs in 2022.

Cole Caufield
Right Wing | 2021–Present

A small but gifted player, Cole Caufield is known for his ability to score goals. Caufield grew up in Wisconsin and played college hockey at the University of Wisconsin. Montreal picked him in the first round of the 2019 NHL Draft. In 2021, Caufield scored four goals in his first 10 NHL games. This included two overtime game-winners scored in back-to-back games. Those were his first two career goals. He scored more than 20 goals in each of his first three full seasons.

Juraj Slafkovský
Left Wing | 2022–Present

The Canadiens selected Juraj Slafkovský with the number one pick in the 2022 NHL Draft. He was born and raised in Slovakia. Slafkovský caught the attention of NHL teams because of his international play. He was the youngest player on the Slovakian national team at the 2022 Winter Olympics and led the tournament in scoring. In the NHL, Slafkovský struggled as a rookie, but he scored 20 goals in his second season.

Mike Matheson
Defenseman | 2022–Present

Montreal's top defenseman, Mike Matheson started his career with the Florida Panthers in 2016. After five seasons in Florida, he then spent two seasons with the Pittsburgh Penguins. The Canadiens traded for him in 2022. Even though Matheson missed 34 games with an abdominal injury, he scored 96 points in his first two seasons in Montreal, more than he scored in all five years with Florida combined.

Maurice Richard was the first player in NHL history to score 500 career goals.

The G.O.A.T.

Maurice "Rocket" Richard is the greatest goal scorer in Montreal Canadiens history. No other Hab has scored more than Richard's 544 goals. Richard was skilled at putting the puck in the net. In 1944–1945, he became the first player in NHL history to score 50 goals in 50 games. In the 80 seasons since he accomplished the feat, only four other players have done this—Mike Bossy, Wayne Gretzky, Mario Lemieux, and Brett Hull. Richard led the NHL in goals scored four more times. The current award for the league's top goal scorer is named the Maurice Richard Trophy.

Fan Favorite

Chris Nilan was one of the toughest players in NHL history. "Knuckles" Nilan was adored by Montreal fans in 1979–1988 as the team's enforcer. Nilan led the NHL in penalty minutes in both 1983–1984 and 1984–1985, but he also had good goal-scoring skills for a tough guy. In 1984–1985, Nilan had a career high in both goals, with 21, and penalty minutes, with 358. He was a key part of the 1986 Stanley Cup-winning team.

The Big Game

On December 31, 1975, the Canadiens played an epic game against the Soviet Union's Red Army team. Many call it one of the best games in hockey history. At this time in history, Russia controlled many territories that were once independent countries. This collection of territories was known as the Soviet Union. The Soviet Union was a major political rival of the US, and both sides would do anything to win. The Canadiens played the better game, even though the Soviet team included some of the world's best players. Montreal had 38 shots while the Soviet Union had only 13. However, Soviet goalie Vladislav Tretiak was outstanding, making 35 saves to manage a 3–3 tie for his team.

Vladislav Tretiak, one of the best goalies of all time, poses with Montreal players after their 1975 game.

Pete Mahovlich earned a total of 569 points during his nine seasons with the Canadiens.

Amazing Feats

Shutouts
In 1928–1929, Canadiens goalie George Hainsworth had 22 shutouts in 44 games. This is both a team and an NHL record.

22

Goals
Three-time All-Star winger Steve Shutt scored 60 goals in the 1976–1977 season. His teammate, Guy Lafleur, tied this record the next season.

60

Assists
In 1974–1975, four-time Stanley Cup-winner Pete Mahovlich dished 82 assists to his teammates.

82

Power Play Goals
Power plays are a key to winning in the NHL. In 1966–1967, winger Yvan Cournoyer helped Montreal reach 32 wins with his 20 power play goals.

20

All-Time Best

MOST POINTS
1. Guy Lafleur — 1,246
2. Jean Béliveau — 1,219
3. Henri Richard — 1,046
4. Maurice Richard — 966
5. Larry Robinson — 883

MOST GOALS
1. Maurice Richard — 544
2. Guy Lafleur — 518
3. Jean Béliveau — 507
4. Yvan Cournoyer — 428
5. Steve Shutt — 408

MOST ASSISTS
1. Guy Lafleur — 728
2. Jean Béliveau — 712
3. Henri Richard — 688
4. Larry Robinson — 686
5. Jacques Lemaire — 469

MOST WINS
1. Carey Price — 361
2. Jacques Plante — 314
3. Patrick Roy — 289
4. Ken Dryden — 258
5. Bill Durnan — 208

HIGHEST SAVE %
1. Ken Dryden — .922
2. Cristobal Huet — .920
   Jacques Plante — .920
4. Jaroslav Halák — .919
5. Carey Price — .917

MOST HAT TRICKS
1. Maurice Richard — 26
2. Jean Béliveau — 18
3. Guy Lafleur — 16
4. Newsy Lalonde — 15
5. Bernie Geoffrion — 14
   Howie Morenz — 14

Guy Lafleur was nicknamed *Le Démon Blond* or "the blond demon" because of the way his hair looked as he sped across the ice.

GLOSSARY

All-Star (ALL STAR) An All-Star is a player chosen as one of the best in their sport.

centennial (sen-TEN-nee-ul) A centennial is the 100th anniversary of an event, or the celebration of the event's 100th year.

division (dih-VIZSH-un) A division is a group of teams within the NHL that compete with each other to have the best record each season and advance to the playoffs.

draft (DRAFT) A draft is a yearly event when teams take turns choosing new players. In the NHL, teams can select North American ice hockey players between the ages of 18 and 20 and international players between 18 and 21 to join the league.

dynasty (DIE-nuh-stee) A dynasty is a powerful group, such as a team, that leads or rules for a long period of time.

enforcer (in-FOR-sur) An enforcer in hockey is a strong, physical player whose job is to defend his star teammates on the ice.

Hall of Fame (HAHL of FAYM) The Hockey Hall of Fame is a museum in Ontario, Canada. The best players and coaches in the game are honored there.

heritage (HER-uh-tij) Someone's heritage is a tradition or practice passed down through generations or within a culture.

illegal stick (il-LEE-gul STIK) An illegal stick does not follow the measurements established by league rules. A player caught using an illegal stick receives a two-minute penalty.

penalty (PEN-ul-tee) A penalty in hockey is a consequence for breaking the rules of a game. A player serving a penalty must leave the ice, and their team must continue with one player down.

playoffs (PLAY-offs) Playoffs are games that take place after the end of the regular season to determine each year's championship team.

power play (POW-uhr PLAY) A power occurs when a player gets a penalty and the other team has more players on the ice.

rival (RYE-vuhl) A rival is a team's top competitor, which they try to outdo and play better than each season.

rookie (ROOK-ee) A rookie is a new or first-year player in a professional sport.

FAST FACTS

- The Canadiens almost always play in front of a full house. They once sold out 583 home games in a row!

- Toe Blake was the winningest head coach in Canadiens history. He coached the team from 1955 to 1968 and led Montreal to eight Stanley Cup victories.

- Larry Robinson holds the record for the most playoff games played for the Canadiens, with 203.

- Jean Béliveau has the most playoff points of any Canadiens player, with 176 points throughout his career.

ONE STRIDE FURTHER

- Maurice "Rocket" Richard is one of the greatest players in Canadiens history. His younger brother Henri also had a Hall of Fame career with the Habs. He joined the Canadiens in 1955, which was his brother's 14th season as a Hab. Compare their careers and decide which you think was the better player. List your reasons supporting one or the other.

- Along with traditional statistics, the NHL also records advanced stats. These measure player effectiveness using different metrics, such as Corsi and Zone Starts. Look up these stats for your favorite Habs players. Decide whether looking at them through a new lens changes your opinion about them.

- It is often said that the Stanley Cup is the hardest trophy to win. It involves getting through 82 regular-season games, plus four best-of-seven playoff rounds in a very physical sport. Look at what it takes to win a championship in MLB, the NBA, or the NFL. Explain which one seems toughest to you.

- Ask friends and family members to name their favorite sport to watch and their favorite sport to play. Keep track and make a graph to see which sports are the most popular.

FIND OUT MORE

IN THE LIBRARY

Creamer, Chris and Todd Radom. *Fabric of the Game: The Stories Behind the NHL's Names, Logos, and Uniforms.* New York: Skyhorse Sports Publishing, 2020.

Fickett, Jamie. *The Boston Bruins vs. the Montreal Canadiens.* Coral Springs, FL: Seahorse Publishing, 2024.

Laughlin, Kara L. *Hockey*. Parker, CO: The Child's World, 2024.

ON THE WEB

Visit our website for links about the Montreal Canadiens:

childsworld.com/links

Note to Parents, Caregivers, Teachers, and Librarians: We routinely verify our web links to make sure they are safe and active sites. So encourage your readers to check them out!

INDEX

Atlantic Division 4

Béliveau, Jean 7, 11, 16, 28, 31

Bell Centre 10–11, 13, 15, 20

Caufield, Cole 20

Hall of Fame 7–8, 13, 15–16, 31

Lafleur, Guy 7, 11, 16, 27–28

Matheson, Mike 21

Nilan, Chris 23

Price, Carey 13, 28

Richard, Maurice 22–23, 28, 31

Robinson, Larry 7, 17, 28, 31

Roy, Patrick 13, 17, 19, 28

Slafkovský, Juraj 21

Stanley Cup 4, 6–7, 13, 16–19, 23, 27, 31

Suzuki, Nick 20

Youppi! 15